Charlie the
Cheetah

by Jan Latta

Reading consultant: Susan Nations, M.Ed., author/literacy coach/consultant in literacy development
Science and curriculum consultant: Debra Voege, M.A., science and math curriculum resource teacher

GARETH STEVENS
GS
PUBLISHING
A Member of the WRC Media Family of Companies

Hello! My name is Charlie, and I am a cheetah. I live in the open **grasslands** of Africa with my brother and sister.

Cheetahs have lived on Earth for four million years.
My **ancestors** once lived in North America, Europe,
Africa, and Asia.

Now we only live in Africa and some parts of Asia.

Our fur is tan with black spots. Sometimes people think we are leopards because leopards also have spots.

We are the only animals that have black lines running from our eyes to our mouth. The lines help keep the Sun from shining into our eyes.

I have a brother and a sister. We were all born blind. Four to ten days after birth, we started to see. For the first six weeks, we fed entirely on Mom's milk. Then Mom fed us from the food she caught. She will start teaching us how to hunt when we are six months old. When we are two years old, we will hunt on our own.

Cheetahs are built for speed. I have special paws and claws that grip the ground. My nose, lungs, and heart are extra big so I can breathe in enough **oxygen** to keep running fast.

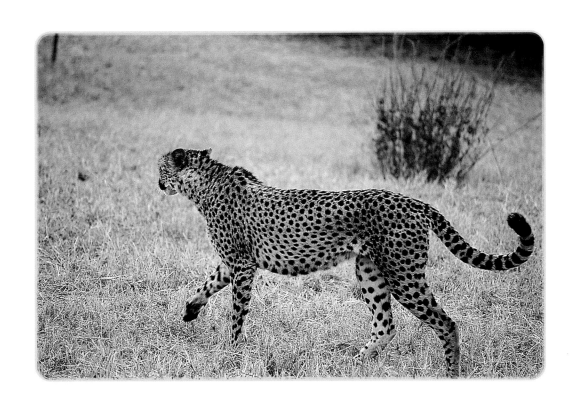

My spine stretches out like a rubber band so I can take long leaps and quickly cover a lot of ground. My long tail helps me keep my balance when I change directions.

Cheetahs are the fastest animals on land. Over a short distance, we can run up to 70 miles (115 kilometers) per hour!

We can cover 23 to 26 feet (7 to 8 meters) in one leap. In just two seconds, we can zoom from 0 to 28 miles (45 km) per hour. We get tired, however, after about 328 feet (100 m).

Cheetahs are **carnivores**, which means we eat other animals. We go to the highest ground on the plains to search for **prey**. We also climb trees to get a better view of our prey.

We hide in the grass to wait for our prey. Then, with a burst of great speed, we start the chase. With one bite to its throat, we kill our prey.

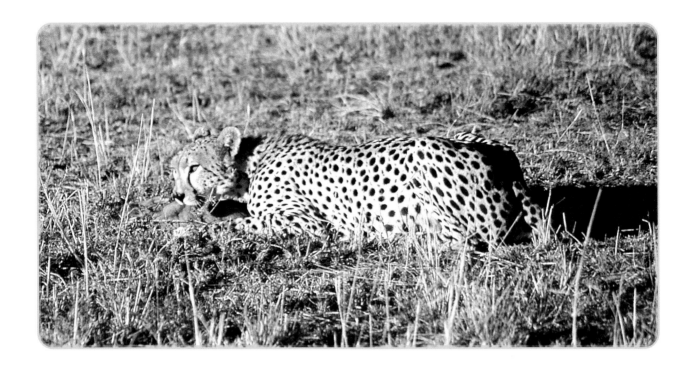

Mom watches over us while we eat. She will protect us from other animals.

After we eat, it is time to get clean. Just like house
cats, we use our rough tongues to **groom** ourselves
and each other.

We use lots of sounds to **communicate**. We hiss,
chirp, growl, bark, yelp, bleat, and purr very loudly.
We never roar like lions or tigers.

Fewer than 12,500 cheetahs are left in the world. We are losing our **habitat** because people build roads, towns, and farms where we live.

Some people kill us for our beautiful fur. Every day is a struggle for our wild animal family to survive. Without help, we cannot outrun **extinction**.

Cheetah Facts

Did You Know?

- Cheetahs live in many countries in Africa. They also live in Iran in Asia.

- Cheetahs usually live in grasslands, but they can also live in forests or on mountains.

- At birth, cheetahs weigh about 9 to 11 ounces (250 to 300 grams). They grow fast. By the time they are adults, they weigh about 80 to 143 pounds (36 to 65 kilograms).

- Cheetahs are about 6 to 7 feet (1.8 to 2.15 meters) long.

- Some cheetahs have black stripes and big, blotchy spots instead of small spots all over. These cheetahs are called King cheetahs.

- Cheetahs eat small antelopes, warthogs, birds, and hares. They will also eat bird eggs and fruit.

- Cheetah mothers must protect their cubs from lions, leopards, and hyenas.

- Cheetahs live about seven years in the wild. They live eight to twelve years in zoos and protected areas.

- From a complete stop, a cheetah can reach its top speed in three seconds.

- Cheetahs have been raced against greyhound dogs. Cheetahs were usually the winners.

- Cheetahs run on their toes. At full speed, there are times when a cheetah's feet do not touch the ground.

- By the time a cheetah catches its prey, it is tired from running. A cheetah usually rests about thirty minutes before eating.

- About three thousand years ago, some wealthy people kept cheetahs as pets.

- About twenty-five hundred cheetahs live in Namibia. That is the largest number of wild cheetahs living in one place.

Map — Where Cheetahs Live

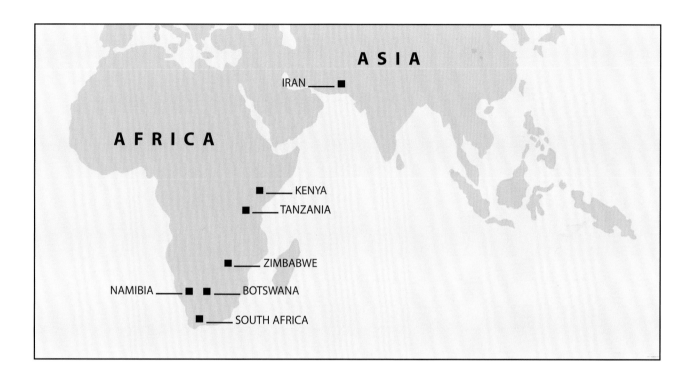

Glossary

ancestors — relatives that lived long before one's parents were born

carnivores — meat eaters

communicate — to send messages to others

extinction — the state of no longer living, or existing

grasslands — large areas of flat land covered with grass

groom — to lick, brush, and clean

habitat — the environment, or place, where an animal lives

oxygen — a gas that all animals breathe in and need to live

prey — animals that are hunted

More Information

Books

Cheetah. Welcome Books (series). Edana Eckart (Children's Press)

Cheetahs. Early Bird Nature Books (series). Barbara Keevil Parker (Lerner Publications)

The Cheetah: Fast as Lightning. Animal Close-Ups (series). Christine Denis-Huot and Michel Denis-Huot (Charlesbridge Publishing)

Web Sites

National Geographic Kids: Cheetahs
www.nationalgeographic.com/kids/creature_feature/0003/cheetah.html
Send a post card, watch a video, hear fun facts about cheetahs, and more.

I'm a Cheetah
www.pbs.org/kratts/world/africa/cheetah
Peek at the creature profile of the world's fastest land mammal.

Publisher's note to educators and parents: Our editors have carefully reviewed these Web sites to ensure that they are suitable for children. Many Web sites change frequently, however, and we cannot guarantee that a site's future contents will continue to meet our high standards of quality and educational value. Be advised that children should be closely supervised whenever they access the Internet.

Please visit our Web site at: **www.garethstevens.com**
For a free color catalog describing Gareth Stevens Publishing's list of high-quality books and multimedia programs, call 1-800-542-2595 (USA) or 1-800-387-3178 (Canada). Gareth Stevens Publishing's fax: (414) 332-3567.

Library of Congress Cataloging-in-Publication Data

Latta, Jan.
  Charlie the cheetah / by Jan Latta. — North American ed.
    p. cm. — (Wild animal families)
  Includes bibliographical references.
  ISBN-13: 978-0-8368-7767-0 (lib. bdg.)
  ISBN-13: 978-0-8368-7774-8 (softcover)
  1. Cheetah—Juvenile literature. I. Title.
QL737.C23L364 2007
599.75'9—dc22   2006032120

This North American edition first published in 2007 by
Gareth Stevens Publishing
A Member of the WRC Media Family of Companies
330 West Olive Street, Suite 100
Milwaukee, WI 53212 USA

This U.S. edition copyright © 2007 by Gareth Stevens, Inc.
Original edition and photographs copyright © 2005 by Jan Latta.
First produced as *Adventures with Chipper the Cheetah* by
TRUE TO LIFE BOOKS, 12b Gibson Street, Bronte, NSW 2024 Australia

Acknowledgements: The author thanks Kathy and Karl Ammann in Africa, who helped make this book possible. And to Jon Resnick who generously allowed reproduction of his photographs on pages 8 and 13.

Project editor: Jan Latta
Design: Jan Latta

Gareth Stevens editorial direction: Valerie J. Weber
Gareth Stevens editor: Tea Benduhn
Gareth Stevens art direction: Tammy West
Gareth Stevens Graphic designer: Scott Krall
Gareth Stevens production: Jessica Yanke and Robert Kraus

Printed in Canada

1 2 3 4 5 6 7 8 9 10 10 09 08 07 06